EXCEPTIONAL LATINOS

SELENA GOMEZ

Superstar Singer and Actress

Maria Betances

Enslow Publishing
101 W. 23rd Street
Suite 240
New York, NY 10011
USA

enslow.com

Words to Know

ambassador—A person who travels to another country to represent a group.

audition—A short performance to show the talents of someone who is being considered for a role.

debut—To present to the public for the first time.

designer—A person who plans how something new will look and be made.

producer—A person who is in charge of making and often providing the money for a play, movie, or record.

solo—Done by a single performer instead of a group.

sound track—The music used in a movie.

Tejano—Tex-Mex music combining elements of traditional, rock, and country music.

Contents

Selena Gomez

CHAPTER 1

Young Actress

Selena Gomez is famous around the world. She is a young Latina of many talents. She is an actress, singer, and fashion **designer**. She worked hard to rise to the top from a young age.

Selena was born on July 22, 1992, in Grand Prairie, Texas. She was named for the **Tejano** singer Selena. Her parents are Amanda "Mandy" Cornett and Ricardo Gomez, whose family is from Mexico.

Selena's parents divorced when she was five. She stayed with her mother. The two did not have much money, and life was not easy. Selena's mother worked three jobs. They often had to buy food at dollar stores and sometimes ran out of gas for their car. Selena still remembers how strong and uncomplaining her mother was during this hard time.

Early Roles

Selena's mother found time to act in plays, though. Selena loved watching her on stage. She told her mother she wanted to act too. In 2002 Selena got her first role. She appeared on a children's television show filmed in Texas called *Barney & Friends*. She acted and sang for two seasons, until **producers** told her she looked too old for her part.

Selena wanted more roles, so she went on many **auditions**. She did not get much work at

On the popular children's show *Barney & Friends*, Selena Gomez (on yellow ball) with Demi Lovato (on blue ball wearing glasses and red headband).

first. Finally, she won a small role in the 2003 movie *Spy Kids 3-D: Game Over* and the 2005 TV movie *Walker, Texas Ranger: Trial by Fire*. In 2006 Selena got a part in a TV show called *Brain Zapped*. She even recorded a song for the show.

Selena Says:

"I was very shy when I was little. I didn't know what 'camera right' was. I didn't know what blocking was. I learned everything from *Barney*."

CHAPTER 2

Big Break

In 2006 Selena got her big break. She was given roles on the successful Disney Channel shows *The Suite Life of Zack and Cody* and *Hannah Montana*. Even though the roles were small, the producers saw that she had star quality.

The next year, Selena won the starring role on the new series *Wizards of Waverly Place*. She played teen witch Alex Russo. "I'm nothing like [Alex]," said Selena. "She's kind of mean and a little bit sassy and I think I'd get in trouble for that."

The show became very popular, and Selena's life got very busy. She woke up at 5 A.M. and worked until 5 P.M. That meant there was no time for her to go to a regular school. Instead, she attended classes on set.

On *Wizards of Waverly Place*, Selena played Alex Russo, a wizard in training.

Selena Says:

"I'm having a blast! I've been blessed with everything that I'm doing."

Rising Star

Even with a successful show, Selena kept looking for new roles. In 2008 her voice was used in the cartoon movie *Horton Hears a Who!* She also starred in the TV movie *Another Cinderella Story*. Selena filmed two movies for the Disney Channel too. She costarred in one, *Princess Protection Program,* with best friend Demi Lovato.

Selena was often involved in the music in the movies and shows she appeared in. She recorded three songs for the **sound track** to *Another Cinderella Story* and sang "One and

Selena was a modern-day Cinderella in the movie
Another Cinderella Story.

the Same" with Demi for *Princess Protection Program*. Selena also recorded four songs for the sound track to *Wizards of Waverly Place: The Movie*.

CHAPTER 3

Musical Debut

Soon Hollywood Records asked Selena to record a whole album. In 2009 Selena and her band, Selena Gomez and the Scene, released *Kiss & Tell*. The album sold well, and the song "Naturally" became a hit. Another album followed in 2010—*A Year Without Rain*. It was an even bigger success with two Top 40 singles: "Round & Round" and "A Year Without Rain."

The group's third album, *When the Sun Goes Down,* had its **debut** at number three on the US Billboard 200 chart in 2011. The singles "Who

Selena with her band, the Scene

Says" and "Love You Like a Love Song" both became Top 40 hits.

A Latina at Heart

Selena's Mexican roots are easy to hear in her music. Some of her albums feature Spanish

Even while performing her music and acting, Selena kept up with her studies. She finished high school in 2010.

songs such as "Un Año Sin Lluvia" on *A Year Without Rain.* She has said that her "dream would be to have an entire album in Spanish." Selena has been studying the Spanish language in recent years to connect more with her father's family in Mexico as well as her many Latino fans.

Selena Says:

"My influences, especially with [*A Year Without Rain*], would be Cheryl Cole from the UK and Katy Perry. The way that they carry themselves and their music styles were very inspiring for me."

CHAPTER 4

So Many Roles

The next few years held different roles for Selena's acting, music, and fashion careers. She was the voice of Mavis in the cartoon movie *Hotel Transylvania* in 2012. Then in 2013 she appeared in the movies *Spring Breakers* and *Getaway*.

Selena decided to go **solo** in her music career, releasing *Stars Dance* in 2013. The album hit number one on the US charts in its first week. "Come & Get It" was her first Top Ten song. In 2014 Selena released an album of her greatest

Selena starred with Ethan Hawke in the 2013 thriller *Getaway*.

hits, along with a new single—"The Heart Wants What It Wants."

Selena has many roles outside of acting and singing too. In 2010 she launched her fashion line Dream Out Loud. It was a great success. Selena said, "All of my hard work has truly paid off. I didn't want to just slap my name on it. I wanted it to be real clothes that real people could wear."

Giving Back

Selena has causes close to her heart too. She is an **ambassador** for UNICEF (United Nations Children's Fund), helping poor and needy children worldwide. She has traveled to Ghana, Chile, and Nepal. She has visited schools and learned about efforts to reduce illnesses among the poor.

Selena's work as a UNICEF ambassador is very important to her. Here she enjoys time with young students in Nepal.

Selena Says:

"The children of Nepal have taught me that with a lot of passion, optimism, and hard work, anything is possible."

Selena was once a little girl in Texas wishing to be an actor. She worked hard for each role she played. She also tirelessly pursued her other loves: music and fashion. Still, she finds time to help others. As she continues to reach her many goals, Selena will remain an inspiration for all those with hopes and dreams of their own.

Timeline

1992—Selena is born on July 22 in Grand Prairie, Texas.

2002—Selena gets her first role in *Barney & Friends*.

2006—Selena lands roles on the Disney shows *The Suite Life of Zack and Cody* and *Hannah Montana*.

2007—Selena begins starring in *Wizards of Waverly Place*.

2008—Selena stars in the TV movie *Another Cinderella Story*.

2009—Selena costars in *Princess Protection Program* with Demi Lovato. Selena becomes an ambassador for UNICEF.

2009—Selena Gomez and the Scene releases *Kiss & Tell*.

2010—Selena launches her clothing line Dream Out Loud.

2013—Selena's solo album *Stars Dance* comes out.

2014—Selena releases her greatest album hits, along with new single "The Heart Wants What It Wants."

Learn More

Books

Burns, Kylie. *Selena Gomez*. New York: Crabtree, 2012.

Nelson, Maria. *Selena Gomez.* New York: Gareth Stevens, 2011.

Schwartz, Heather E. *Selena Gomez.* North Mankato, Minn.: Capstone Press, 2013.

Uschan, Michael V. *Selena Gomez*. Farmington Hills, Mich.: Lucent Books, 2014.

Web Sites

unicefusa.org/supporters/celebrities/ambassadors/ selena-gomez

Provides information about Selena Gomez's work with UNICEF.

selenagomez.com

Selena Gomez's official Web site includes news about acting roles, music, and more.

Index

Published in 2016 by Enslow Publishing, LLC.
101 W. 23rd Street, Suite 240, New York, NY 10011

Copyright © 2016 by Enslow Publishing, LLC.

All rights reserved.

No part of this book may be reproduced by any means without the written permission of the publisher.

Cataloging-in-Publication Data

Betances, Maria.

Selena Gomez: superstar singer and actress / by Maria Betances.

  p. cm. —(Exceptional Latinos)

Includes bibliographical references and index.

ISBN 978-0-7660-6720-2 (library binding)

ISBN 978-0-7660-6718-9 (pbk.)

ISBN 978-0-7660-6719-6 (6-pack)

1. Gomez, Selena,—1992—Juvenile literature. 2. Actors—United States—Biography—Juvenile literature. 3. Singers—United States—Biography—Juvenile literature.
I. Title.

PN2287.G585 B483 2016

791.4302'8092—d23

Printed in the United States of America

To Our Readers: We have done our best to make sure all Web site addresses in this book were active and appropriate when we went to press. However, the author and the publisher have no control over and assume no liability for the material available on those Web sites or on any Web sites they may link to. Any comments or suggestions can be sent by e-mail to customerservice@enslow.com.

Photo Credits: Alyse Gilbert/Young Hollywood/Getty Images Entertainment/Getty Images, p. 4; Criag Sjdoin © DISNEY CHANNEL/courtesy Everett Collection, p. 10; Helga Esteb/Shutterstock.com, p. 14; © Hit Entertainment/courtesy Everett Collection, p. 7; Jason Merritt/Getty Images Entertainment/Getty Images (Selena Gomez), p. 1; PRNewsFoto/U.S. Fund for UNICEF/AP Images, p. 20; JStone/Shutterstock.com, p. 15; s.buckley/Shutterstock.com, p. 18; Toria/Shutterstock.com (blue background); © Warner Premier/courtesy Everett Collection, p. 12.

Cover Credits: Jason Merritt/Getty Images Entertainment/Getty Images (Selena Gomez); Toria/Shutterstock.com (blue background).